MICHELLE
OBAMA

HER ESSENTIAL WISDOM

MICHELLE
OBAMA

HER ESSENTIAL WISDOM

EDITED BY CAROL KELLY-GANGI

FALL RIVER PRESS

New York

To my beloved mother and daughter

FALL RIVER PRESS

New York

An Imprint of Sterling Publishing Co., Inc.
1166 Avenue of the Americas
New York, NY 10036

ISBN 978-1-4351-6937-1

Distributed in Canada by Sterling Publishing Co., Inc.
^{c}/o Canadian Manda Group, 664 Annette Street
Toronto, Ontario M6S 2C8, Canada
Distributed in the United Kingdom by GMC Distribution Services
Castle Place, 166 High Street, Lewes, East Sussex BN7 1XU, England
Distributed in Australia by NewSouth Books
University of New South Wales, Sydney, NSW 2052, Australia

For information about custom editions, special sales, and premium and
corporate purchases, please contact Sterling Special Sales at 800-805-5489
or specialsales@sterlingpublishing.com.

Manufactured in the United States of America

4 6 8 10 9 7 5

sterlingpublishing.com

Jacket design by David Ter-Avanesyan

Photo credits: **Flickr: Steve Jurvetson:** 46; **Getty Images/Wire Images:** Paul Zimmerman/
Contributor: cover; **National Archives and Records Administration:** Samantha Appleton: 88;
Sonya N. Hebert: 62, 130; Lawrence Jackson: endpapers, 122; Chuck Kennedy: vi, 10, 18, 104,
112; Amanda Lucidon: 82; Pete Souza: 28, 34, 52, 72, 96; **Princeton University:** x

CONTENTS

INTRODUCTION

It comes as no surprise to the millions of people all over the world who hold Michelle Obama in the highest esteem that she was voted the most admired woman in 2018 according to a December 2018 Gallup poll. She was a groundbreaking First Lady who worked tirelessly for the causes closest to her heart, including women's rights, education, children's health and well-being, and support for the military community. Since leaving the White House, she has continued to work for these causes and others with the same strength, determination, and grace that she embodied as First Lady.

Michelle Obama: Her Essential Wisdom gathers together hundreds of memorable quotations from this remarkable woman. The selections have been carefully collected from her speeches, conferences, summits, interviews, tweets, social media posts, and other writings. Arranged thematically, the excerpts reveal her keen intellect, steadfast determination, and deep compassion, as well as the integrity, candor, and dignity that she has displayed throughout her incredible public life.

In the excerpts, Mrs. Obama shares her deeply held views about America and her steadfast belief in the American ideals of freedom, equality, and justice, which she and her husband have continually striven to promote. She speaks passionately about the essential need for quality education for children and young people at home and around the globe. In other excerpts, she shares her insights into the struggles that all women face and the particular challenges for women of color. She also offers practical advice for young people, and especially for girls, on the subjects of education, empowerment, and success. Elsewhere, she reflects on the value of hardship, the challenges of racism, the realities of politics, and the need for hope in our lives and in our world.

Many excerpts offer insight into a more personal side of Michelle Obama. She speaks lovingly of her parents and how they each taught and guided her throughout her life. She reveals her deep love and admiration for her husband, as well as the hard work they've put into their marriage. She shares her devotion to her daughters, Malia and Sasha, and her pride and joy at the women they are becoming. Another chapter provides a glimpse into her wry sense of humor and offers pragmatic wisdom on subjects such as staying true to yourself, dealing with negativity, and handling social media. The final chapter gathers quotations from writers, feminists, artists, designers, family, and friends, who share their thoughtful insights into Michelle Obama and her living legacy.

Michelle Obama: Her Essential Wisdom invites readers to experience the powerful words of this extraordinary woman who continues to inspire and challenge us to embrace our own best selves.

—CAROL KELLY-GANGI
2019

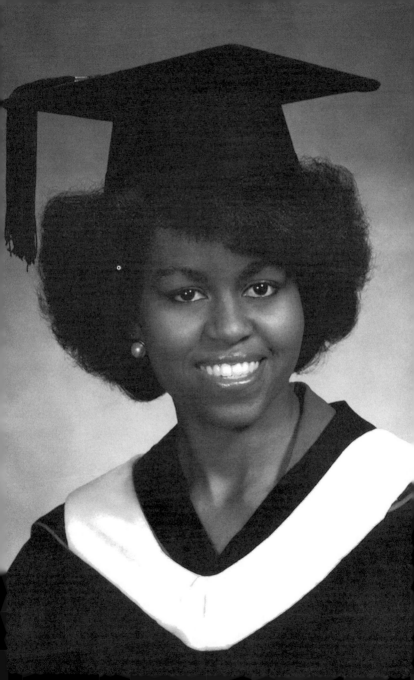

EARLY YEARS

I am an example of what's possible when girls from the very beginning of their lives are loved and nurtured by the people around them. I was surrounded by extraordinary women in my life: grandmothers, teachers, aunts, cousins, neighbors, who taught me about quiet strength and dignity.

—TED Talk, Elizabeth G. Anderson School, London,
April 2, 2009

❧

My family was my world, the center of everything. My mother taught me how to read early, walking me to the public library, sitting with me as I sounded out words on a page. My father went to work every day dressed in the blue uniform of a city laborer, but at night he showed us what it meant to love jazz and art.

—*Becoming*

❧

At 6-foot-6, I've often felt like Craig was looking down on me too . . . literally. But the truth is, both when we were kids and today, he wasn't looking down on me—he was watching over me.

—On her brother Craig Robinson, Democratic National Convention,
Denver, Colorado, August 25, 2008

Getting good grades was always important to me, and it wasn't because my parents were hounding me or that they had the expectation. It was something that I wanted for myself. I wanted an A, you know, I wanted to be smart, I wanted to be the person who had the right answer.

—Women's History Month Event, Washington, D.C.,
March 19, 2009

☙

I grew up in a working class family in Chicago. And while neither of my parents went past high school, let me tell you, they saved up every penny that my dad earned at his city job because they were determined to send me to college.

—Commencement address, City College of New York,
June 3, 2016

☙

You see, Barack and I were both raised by families who didn't have much in the way of money or material possessions but who had given us something far more valuable—their unconditional love, their unflinching sacrifice, and the chance to go places they had never imagined for themselves.

—Democratic National Convention, Charlotte, North Carolina,
September 4, 2012

[G]rowing up as a black girl on the South Side of Chicago, where the expectations of me were limited, as I was trying to make my way and do good in school and apply to good colleges, there were always people around telling me what I couldn't do, always telling me how far I should only dream. And my reaction to that at that time was to prove the doubters wrong. That spurred me—"I'll show you." They give you strength.

—South by Southwest Music Festival,
Austin, Texas, March 16, 2016

When I was a teenager, a high school counselor of mine took one look at me and decided I wouldn't be able to cut it in the Ivy League. It's one of those moments that, I realize now, could have broken me. . . . What I did was channel that hurt into a singular focus on getting into Princeton and proving that counselor wrong.

—Interview, *Ebony*, December 2018

What mattered was what was in my mind and what was in my heart. So my four years in school gave me the confidence to know that if I could make it on a college campus, I could make it anywhere.

—Commencement address, Eastern Kentucky University,
Richmond, Kentucky, May 11, 2013

It was the first time I had been in a predominantly white situation. So I had to learn how to adjust in this new world of wealth and privilege and kids that I didn't realize had come from prep schools that had prepared them. And I didn't even know the language of that college. What was a syllabus? Never heard of it.

— *Interview, "Becoming Michelle: A First Lady's Journey with Robin Roberts," November 11, 2018*

And I decided to rise. Yes, I decided to rewrite those tired old scripts that define too many of us. I decided that I wasn't bossy—I was confident and strong. I wasn't loud—I was a young woman with something important to say. And when I looked into the mirror, I saw a tall and smart and beautiful black girl. And that, more than anything else, is what I want all of you to know. I want that for you. I want you to live life on your own terms, according to your own script.

—BET's "Black Girls Rock!" event, Newark, New Jersey,
March 28, 2015

After graduating from college, we did everything we thought we should do to be successful—Craig went to business school, I went to law school, we got prestigious jobs at an investment bank and me at a law firm. We soon had all the traditional markers of success: the fat paycheck, the fancy office, the impressive lines on our resumés. But the truth is, neither of us was all that fulfilled. I didn't want to be up in some tall office building writing legal memos. I wanted to be down on the ground helping the folks I grew up with. I was living the dream, but it wasn't my dream.

—Commencement address, Oregon State University,
Corvallis, Oregon, June 17, 2012

I had a mom and dad who gave me the skills to channel my frustration into something productive. They instilled in me a sense of my own worth, the belief that my goals were achievable. And most important, they taught me to focus on controlling the things I could control, and not to worry about the things I couldn't.

—Interview, *Ebony*, December 2018

ॐ

There is just a sense of security that allows you to take risks. People think that it comes from wealth or generations of access and success, but it doesn't. The security of your parents' love really gives you the foundation to think you can fly. And then you do.

—Interview, *Essence*, May 2009

ॐ

He was very straightforward. He wasn't playin' games. I say that to the ladies out there. Not a game player. Very clear about what he wanted. When we stopped for ice cream and he got the sense that I was starting to open up. And he, you know, he played it real smooth. He just leaned in for a kiss. And that really was it. You know, from that kiss on, we were—it was—it was love. And he was my man.

—Interview, "Becoming Michelle: A First Lady's Journey with Robin Roberts," November 11, 2018

I left the practice of law to go into public service for selfish reasons. I wanted to be happy and feel good every single day. I wanted to wake up inspired and ready to do something greater than myself.

—United State of Women Summit, Washington, D.C.,
June 14, 2016

Life was you get married, you have kids, you buy a home. I thought Barack would be a partner at a law firm or maybe teach or work in the community. We'd watch our kids go to college and go to their weddings and take care of the grandkids and that was it.

—Interview, *People*, August 4, 2008

EDUCATION AND EMPOWERMENT

[E]ducation is a very personal thing for me. As I tell girls whenever I meet them, I wouldn't be here, sitting here not just in this chair but in the life that I have, if it weren't for my education. I know that when you hear the phrase "knowledge is power," it's true.

—*Glamour*'s "A Brighter Future: A Global Conversation on Girls' Education," Washington, D.C., October 11, 2016

❧

The ability to read, write, and analyze; the confidence to stand up and demand justice and equality; the qualifications and connections to get your foot in that door and take your seat at that table—all of that starts with education. And trust me, girls around the world, they understand this. They feel it in their bones, and they will do whatever it takes to get that education.

—"Let Girls Learn" event celebrating International Women's Day, Washington, D.C., March 8, 2016

❧

If you want to know the reason why I'm standing here, it's because of education. I never cut class. Sorry, I don't know if anybody here is cutting class. I never did it. I loved getting As. I liked being smart. I loved being on time. I loved getting my work done. I thought being smart was cooler than anything in the world. And you too, with these same values, can control your own destiny. You too can pave the way. You too can realize your dreams, and then your job is to reach back and to help someone just like you do the same thing.

—TED Talk, Elizabeth G. Anderson School, London, April 2, 2009

We wanted to change the conversation around what it means and what it takes to be a success in this country. Because let's be honest, if we're always shining the spotlight on professional athletes or recording artists or Hollywood celebrities, if those are the only achievements we celebrate, then why would we ever think kids would see college as a priority?

—Final remarks as First Lady, School Counselor of the Year Ceremony,
Washington, D.C., January 6, 2017

∿

As I've said many times before, arts education is not a luxury, it's a necessity. It's really the air many of these kids breathe. It's how we get kids excited about getting up and going to school in the morning. It's how we get them to take ownership of their future. And, most importantly, it's how we get [them] to go to college.

—National Arts and Humanities Youth Program Awards,
Washington, D.C., November 17, 2015

∿

And I can't say this enough here, but the arts cannot be an option for our kids. It's got to be a necessity, just like math and science and reading, and all that kind of stuff. Arts has to be a part of that, because we know that students who get involved in things like music or drama or visual arts, they just do better. The studies are clear. They have better grades, they have better graduation rates, they have better college enrollment rates. Music and arts is a foundation for an outstanding education.

—Jazz Festival Workshop, Washington, D.C.,
April 29, 2016

You have to stay in school. You have to. You have to go to college. You have to get your degree. Because that's the one thing people can't take away from you, is your education. And it is worth the investment.

—National Arts and Humanities Youth Program Awards,
Washington, D.C., November 15, 2016

❧

We're seeking to empower adolescent girls around the world through education, so that they can support their families, communities and countries. The evidence is clear. Girls who attend secondary school earn higher salaries, have lower infant and maternal mortality rates, and are less likely to contract malaria and HIV. And studies have shown that educating girls isn't just good for the girls, it's good for all of us.

—CNN op-ed upon the launch of the Global Girls Alliance,
October 11, 2018

❧

If we want to end poverty, global poverty, if we want to improve the plight of our country—educating girls is the key to all of that. It just is.

—"Let Girls Learn" event, New York City,
September 29, 2015

The future of our world is only as bright as the future of our girls.

—CNN op-ed upon the launch of the Global Girls Alliance,
October 11, 2018

❧

Today, I'm free. I'm really free because I have an education—not because I'm First Lady, because I have an education. So if you want to be like me, I want you all to focus in school. I want you to put down your phones—a little bit more.

—*Hidden Figures* film screening, Washington, D.C.,
December 15, 2016

❧

At the foundation of everything we have all done, it's understanding that education is key. That's the thing in your life that you have complete control over. You can go to school and focus—not just be there, but actually put effort into it. Go to your classes. Study hard. Do your best. Get your homework done. Go to college.

—Love and Happiness Concert: Student Workshop,
Washington, D.C., October 21, 2016

❧

Public education is our greatest pathway to opportunity in America. So we need to invest in and strengthen our public universities today, and for generations to come.

—Commencement address, City College of New York,
June 3, 2016

If the school in your neighborhood isn't any good, don't just accept it. Get in there, fix it. Talk to the parents. Talk to the teachers. Get business and community leaders involved as well, because we all have a stake in building schools worthy of our children's promise.

—*Commencement address, Bowie State University, College Park, Maryland, May 17, 2013*

All of these young people have some kind of potential in them. And if we don't invest in them as a nation, regardless of where they come from or what color they are, if we don't invest in them, we lose. Imagine this talent bottled up in these kids unexplored, uninvested. There are millions of kids like this in this country who do not have the resources to become everything that they could be. And shame on us if we can't do this better.

—**National Arts and Humanities Youth Program Awards,**
Washington, D.C., November 15, 2016

∿

As you start this new school year, I want you to strive to work harder than ever before, challenge yourself to reach new heights, and seek new opportunities that will help you grow. I believe in you!

@MichelleObama, Twitter, August 28, 2018

AMERICA

I stand here today at the crosscurrents of that history—knowing
that my piece of the American Dream is a blessing hard won
by those who came before me. All of them driven by the same
conviction that drove my dad to get up an hour early each day
to painstakingly dress himself for work. The same conviction that
drives the men and women I've met all across this country. . . .
All of us driven by a simple belief that the world as it is just won't
do—that we have an obligation to fight for the world as it should
be. And that is the thread that connects our hearts. That is the
thread that runs through my journey and Barack's journey and so
many other improbable journeys that have brought us here tonight,
where the current of history meets this new tide of hope. That is
why I love this country.

—Democratic National Convention, Denver, Colorado,
August 25, 2008

﹏

Whether it's climate change or cancer or ending hunger, by seeking
out the most talented, passionate, skilled people we can find and
putting them to work, regardless of what they look like or where
they come from or how they pray or who they love, that's how we
become the best America that we can be.

—*Hidden Figures* film screening, Washington, D.C.,
December 15, 2016

Like so many American families, our families weren't asking for much. They didn't begrudge anyone else's success or care that others had much more than they did. In fact, they admired it. They simply believed in that fundamental American promise that, even if you don't start out with much, if you work hard and do what you're supposed to do, then you should be able to build a decent life for yourself and an even better life for your kids and grandkids.

—Democratic National Convention, Charlotte,
North Carolina, September 4, 2012

That is the story of this country, the story that has brought me to this stage tonight, the story of generations of people who felt the lash of bondage, the shame of servitude, the sting of segregation, but who kept on striving and hoping and doing what needed to be done so that today I wake up every morning in a house that was built by slaves.

—Democratic National Convention, Philadelphia,
July 25, 2016

Our history is one long testament to the fundamental truth that real change doesn't come from the top down from Washington, it comes from the bottom up—from citizens organizing and mobilizing and serving the nation that they love.

—National Conference on Volunteering and Service
in San Francisco, June 22, 2009

Because that's what we do in America—a country where a girl like me from the South Side of Chicago, whose great-great grandfather was a slave, can graduate from some of the finest universities on Earth. We live in a country where a biracial kid from Hawaii who was the son of a single mother can become president. We live in a country that has always been a beacon for people who have come to our shores and poured their hopes, and their prayers, and their backbreaking hard work into making us who we are today.

—Campaign speech, Philadelphia,
September 28, 2016

∾

That is the power of our differences to make us smarter and more creative. And that is how all those infusions of new cultures and ideas, generation after generation, created the matchless alchemy of our melting pot and helped us build the strongest, most vibrant, most prosperous nation on the planet, right here.

—Commencement address, City College of New York,
June 3, 2016

∾

And in my own life, in my own small way, I've tried to give back to this country that has given me so much. That's why I left a job at a law firm for a career in public service, working to empower young people to volunteer in their communities. Because I believe that each of us—no matter what our age or background or walk of life— each of us has something to contribute to the life of this nation.

—Democratic National Convention, Denver, Colorado,
August 25, 2008

It's about leaving something better for our kids. That's how we've always moved this country forward, by all of us coming together on behalf of our children, folks who volunteer to coach that team, to teach that Sunday school class, because they know it takes a village.

—Democratic National Convention,
Philadelphia, July 25, 2016

❧

And here in America, we don't give in to our fears. We don't build up walls to keep people out because we know that our greatness has always depended on contributions from people who were born elsewhere but sought out this country and made it their home— from innovations like Google and eBay to inventions like the artificial heart, the telephone, even the blue jeans; to beloved patriotic songs like "God Bless America," like national landmarks like the Brooklyn Bridge and, yes, the White House—both of which were designed by architects who were immigrants.

—Commencement address, City College of New York,
June 3, 2016

❧

I am making my mark in hopes that my grandchildren will experience something better than I did, just as my parents laid down markers so that my life would be better than theirs. We don't fix things in a lifetime. There have been harder times in our nation's history than this.

—Interview, NPR, November 9, 2018

If you are a person of faith, know that religious diversity is a great American tradition, too. In fact, that's why people first came to this country—to worship freely. And whether you are Muslim, Christian, Jewish, Hindu, Sikh—these religions are teaching our young people about justice, and compassion, and honesty. So I want our young people to continue to learn and practice those values with pride. You see, our glorious diversity—our diversities of faiths and colors and creeds—that is not a threat to who we are, it makes us who we are.

—Final remarks as First Lady, School Counselor of the Year Ceremony,
Washington, D.C., January 6, 2017

❧

We are a nation founded as a rebuke to tyranny. A nation of revolutionaries who refused sovereign reign from afar. Hear me—we're a nation that says give us your tired, your poor, your huddled masses yearning to breathe free. A nation built on our differences, guided by the belief that we're all created equal. A nation that fully recognizes that we are always stronger together—all of us. That's who we are.

—Campaign speech, Phoenix, Arizona,
October 20, 2016

The people in this country are universally good and kind and honest and decent. Don't be afraid of the country you live in. The folks here are good.

—30th Anniversary of the Women's
Foundation of Colorado,
Denver, July 25, 2017

[F]or the past eight years, I have had the great honor of being this country's First Lady. First Ladies, we rock. But I have traveled from one end of this country to the other, and I have met people from every conceivable background and walk of life, including folks who disagree with just about everything Barack and I have ever said, but who welcome us into their communities. Remember, our neighbors are decent folks. These are all good people, who are open-hearted and willing to listen. And while we might not change each other's minds, we always walk away reminded that when it comes to what really matters, when it comes to our hopes and dreams for our children, we're just not all that different.

—Campaign speech, Winston-Salem, North Carolina,
October 27, 2016

༄

So for all the young people in this room and those who are watching, know that this country belongs to you—to all of you, from every background and walk of life. If you or your parents are immigrants, know that you are part of a proud American tradition—the infusion of new cultures, talents and ideas, generation after generation, that has made us the greatest country on earth.

—Final remarks as First Lady, School Counselor of the Year Ceremony,
Washington, D.C., January 6, 2017

FREEDOM, RIGHTS, JUSTICE, AND EQUALITY

You cannot take your freedoms for granted. Just like generations who have come before you, you have to do your part to preserve and protect those freedoms. . . . [Y]ou need to be preparing yourself to add your voice to our national conversation. You need to prepare yourself to be informed and engaged as a citizen, to serve and to lead, to stand up for our proud American values and to honor them in your daily lives.

—Final remarks as First Lady, School Counselor of the Year Ceremony, Washington, D.C., January 6, 2017

❧

I want you to remember that folks marched and protested for our right to vote. They endured beatings and jail time, they sacrificed their lives for this right. So I know you can get yourselves to the polls and exercise that right. Because make no mistake about it, casting our vote is the ultimate way we go high when they go low. Voting is our high. That's how we go high: We vote.

—Campaign speech, Winston-Salem, North Carolina, October 27, 2016

❧

But here's the problem, while some folks are frustrated and tuned out and staying home on Election Day, trust me, other folks are showing up. Democracy continues with or without you.

—Campaign speech during the 2018 midterm elections, Las Vegas, September 24, 2018

It's amazing to me that we still have to tell people about the importance of voting. You know, that almost every two years, we're having this conversation to get people to the polls. And in the end, that's how our democracy works. People have to be educated, they have to be focused on the issues and they have to go to the polls if they want their politics to reflect their values.

—Interview, "Becoming Michelle: A First Lady's Journey
with Robin Roberts," November 11, 2018

∾

Thank you to every single one of you who made your voice heard, volunteered, and reached out to your neighbors. You proved that we have the power to change this country—and that every single vote counts. Now it's up to us to keep building this movement. We've only just begun.

@MichelleObama, Twitter, November 7, 2018

∾

Dr. King understood. . . that one of the surest paths to progress here in America runs straight through the voting booth. That's been the key to every single stride we have ever taken in this country—from fighting discrimination to passing health care. It all starts with the ballot.

—Commencement address, Jackson State University,
Jackson, Mississippi, April 23, 2016

These issues aren't settled. These freedoms that we take for granted aren't guaranteed in stone. And they certainly didn't just come down to us as a gift from the heavens. No, these rights were secured through long, hard battles waged by women and men who marched, and protested, and made their voices heard in courtrooms and boardrooms and voting booths and the halls of Congress.

—"Let Girls Learn" event celebrating International Women's Day, Washington, D.C., March 8, 2016

That is the well-worn path to Dr. King's mountaintop that so many men and women before us have taken—famous civil rights leaders and ordinary folks who faced down dogs, and batons, and firehoses with prayer and hope and steadfast determination. For as Dr. King told us, he said, "Darkness cannot drive out darkness; only light can do that. Hate cannot drive out hate; only love can do that."

—Commencement address, Jackson State University, Jackson, Mississippi, April 23, 2016

[L]ike most women, I know how it feels to be overlooked, to be underestimated, to have someone only half listen to your ideas at a meeting—to see them turn to the man next to you, the man you supervise, and assume he's in charge—or to experience those whistles and taunts as you walk down the street.

—"Let Girls Learn" event celebrating International Women's Day, Washington, D.C., March 8, 2016

This is an important issue for millions of Americans, and for Barack and me, it really comes down to the values of fairness and equality we want to pass down to our girls. These are basic values that kids learn at a very young age and that we encourage them to apply in all areas of their lives. And in a country where we teach our children that everyone is equal under the law, discriminating against same-sex couples just isn't right. It's as simple as that.

—"First Lady Michelle Obama Answers Your Twitter Questions,"
May 31, 2012

∾

When you've worked hard, and done well, and walked through that doorway of opportunity. . . you do not slam it shut behind you. You reach back, and you give other folks the same chances that helped you succeed.

—Democratic National Convention, Charlotte, North Carolina,
September 4, 2012

WOMEN AND MEN

[O]ur first job in life as women, I think, is to get to know ourselves. And I think a lot of times we don't do that. We spend our time pleasing, satisfying, looking out into the world to define who we are—listening to the messages, the images, the limited definitions that people have of who we are. And that's true for women of color for sure. There is a limited box that we are put in, and if we live by that limited definition we miss out on a lot of who we are.

—United State of Women Summit, Washington, D.C.,
June 14, 2016

❧

That's what these women and girls have to do. Sometimes we have to be better. Sometimes we have to work harder. Sometimes we have to work to combat those negative thoughts in our heads about who we are, and how we look, and what people think about us. So many of us, as women and girls, we are haunted by the voices of other people who tell us what we can't do. And it's something that you have to work on every single day. Every woman that you know is working on this. I am still working on it. And it takes being conscious of the fact that these voices are there, and they can hold you back. But you've got to push through them.

—*Glamour*'s "A Brighter Future: A Global Conversation on
Girls' Education," Washington, D.C., October 11, 2016

The difference between a struggling family and a healthy one is often the presence of an empowered woman or women at the center of that family. The difference between a broken community and a thriving one is often the healthy respect between men and women who appreciate the contributions each other makes to society. The difference between a languishing nation and one that will flourish is the recognition that we need equal access to education for both boys and girls.

—TED Talk, Elizabeth G. Anderson School, London,
April 2, 2009

∾

And if we really want to honor these girls, like Malala, and like the girls in Nigeria, and girls in Tanzania, who would give anything to get an education, then the very first thing we have to do is take our education seriously and not take it for granted, to be that voice. Because it's going to be up to the girls to get that education so they can be the fighters, and the champions, and the policymakers, and the next generation of world leaders who are going to make these changes.

—*Glamour*'s "A Brighter Future: A Global Conversation on
Girls' Education," Washington, D.C., October 11, 2016

∾

They're charging forwards in sports and maths and science and technology. They're speaking up and speaking out, not just in classrooms but in the public arena at a young age. I find great hope in this generation of young women.

—Interview, *Good Housekeeping*, January 2019

[L]et me tell you, to compete in school, in schools where boys are given the benefit of the doubt, you're going to have to be aggressive. And you've got to be confident. And there are times when you need to be loud and speak your mind. I've had to do that in every room of power that I've sat in, and I've had to learn that my voice has value. And if I don't use it, what's the point of me being in the room?

—*Glamour*'s "A Brighter Future: A Global Conversation on Girls' Education," Washington, D.C., October 11, 2016

∽

I tried not to feel intimidated when classroom conversation was dominated by male students, which it often was. Hearing them, I realized that they weren't at all smarter than the rest of us. They were simply emboldened, floating on an ancient tide of superiority, buoyed by the fact that history had never told them anything different.

—*Becoming*

∽

Cute's good, but cute only lasts for so long, and then it's, Who are you as a person? That's the advice I would give to women: Look at the heart. Look at the soul. Look at how the guy treats his mother and what he says about women. How he acts with children he doesn't know. And, more important, how does he treat you? When you're dating a man you should always feel good. You should never feel less than. You should never doubt yourself. You shouldn't be in a relationship with somebody who doesn't make you completely happy and make you feel whole.

—Interview, *Glamour*, December 2009

Be better at everything. Be better fathers. Good lord, just being good fathers who love your daughters and are providing a solid example of what it means to be a good man in the world, showing them what it feels like to be loved. That is the greatest gift that the men in my life gave to me.

—*United State of Women Summit, Washington, D.C.,*
June 14, 2016

When a father puts in long hours at work, he's praised for being dedicated and ambitious. But when a mother stays late at the office, she's sometimes accused of being selfish, neglecting her kids.

—"Let Girls Learn" event, Madrid, Spain, June 30, 2016

❧

It wasn't so long ago that I was a working mom myself. And I know that sometimes, much as we all hate to admit it, it's just easier to park the kids in front of the TV for a few hours, so we can pay the bills or do the laundry or just have some peace and quiet for a change.

—"Let's Move!" anniversary event, Alpharetta, Georgia, February 9, 2011

❧

It's up to all of you to start making those small but meaningful changes in your daily lives that can slowly start to change our norms. One small example: You can start with how you raise your own children if you choose to have them. Maybe it means telling your sons that it's okay to cry, and your daughters that it's okay to be bossy. Maybe it means encouraging your daughters, not just your son, to study math and science and sign up for the football team. And if there isn't a team for girls, maybe it means asking why not.

—"Let Girls Learn" event, Madrid, Spain, June 30, 2016

Women, we endure those cuts in so many ways that we don't even notice we're cut. We are living with small tiny cuts, and we are bleeding every single day. And we're still getting up.

—30th Anniversary of the Women's Foundation of Colorado,
Denver, July 25, 2017

When I get up and work out, I'm working out just as much for my girls as I am for me, because I want them to see a mother who loves them dearly, who invests in them, but who also invests in herself. It's just as much about letting them know as young women that it is okay to put yourself a little higher on your priority list.

—Interview, *Prevention*, March 2012

The men in my life taught me some important things, as well. They taught me about what a respectful relationship should look like between men and women. They taught me about what a strong marriage feels like: that it's built on faith and commitment and an admiration for each other's unique gifts. They taught me about what it means to be a father and to raise a family. And not only to invest in your own home but to reach out and help raise kids in the broader community.

—TED Talk, Elizabeth G. Anderson School, London,
April 2, 2009

We were not put on this Earth just to be good mothers or good wives; we were here to be good citizens and good individuals. And that takes investment. And I want girls to start practicing that at a very early age— not being so selfless that they can't look out for themselves.

—Glamour's *"A Brighter Future: A Global Conversation on Girls' Education," Washington, D.C., October 11, 2016*

[W]e're sometimes taught in our societies that we have to compete and we have to hold each other back in order for one of us to succeed. That is not true. We need each other. And all over the world, we have to be a team of women and girls who love each other and value each other and cherish one another. Because if we don't cherish each other, no one else will.

—*Glamour*'s "A Brighter Future: A Global Conversation on Girls' Education," Washington, D.C., October 11, 2016

❧

So the question is what are you going to do? How are you going to be better? What are you going to change in your office, in your life, in your relationships? What are you going to change in your family dynamic? And how are you going to empower yourself with the knowledge that you need to know what work needs to be done? We can't afford to be ignorant. We can't afford to be complacent. So we have to continue the work.

—United State of Women Summit, Washington, D.C., June 14, 2016

❧

Strong men, men who are truly role models, don't need to put down women to make themselves feel powerful.

—Campaign speech, Manchester, New Hampshire, October 13, 2016

So what I'd say to anyone uncertain about choosing a partner is to take seriously the things you see while you're dating—the good and the bad. And if you really respect each other as individuals, if you can laugh when little things go wrong, if you've had some success working together through some of the tangled knots that spring up in every relationship, then you've got a good start on building a relationship that can last.

—Interview, *Essence*, January 2019

❧

For me, being a mother made me a better professional, because coming home every night to my girls reminded me what I was working for. And being a professional made me a better mother, because by pursuing my dreams, I was modeling for my girls how to pursue *their* dreams.

—"Let Girls Learn" event, Tokyo, March 18, 2015

❧

We've all got to practice self-care, whatever that means to you. It might be carving out some time for exercise, maybe taking an evening walk or doing some yoga in your bedroom before anybody else wakes up. . . . The point is that you've got to take a moment, maybe once a day, maybe once a week, to just say, "I'm sorry, everybody, but I'm doing this for me." You're no good to anyone if you're no good to yourself.

—Interview, *Essence*, January 2019

THE 2008 PRESIDENTIAL ELECTION

I always joke that I took off my "me" hat and put on my "us" hat. And I started thinking about where I would hope to see the country go for my girls. Then I started thinking about the type of person that I want to see in politics. And that always turned out to be a guy like Barack.

—Interview, *Good Housekeeping*, September 30, 2008

❧

I tell people that in our politics we measure by this very narrow definition. And a lot of times it's years in Washington, or whether you've made a lot of money running a very large corporation. I mean, we just tend to weigh certain experiences more than others. But what I say is that the measure of leadership is the choices that people made over a lifetime, not when everybody's looking.

—Interview with Katie Couric, February 14, 2008

❧

[W]e're in some tough times now. And what we can see from the fall of this economy is that when we fall, we all fall. And when we rise, we all rise. And whether we're Republicans or Democrats or Independents, or black or white or straight or gay, that we're in this together. And that there are times that we will disagree, that we won't share the same policies. But, we're going to rise and fall together.

—Interview, *Larry King Live*, October 8, 2008

We're not going to keep running and running and running, because at some point you do get the life beaten out of you. It hasn't been beaten out of us yet. We need to be in there now, while we're still fresh and open and fearless and bold. You lose some of that over time. Barack is not cautious yet; he's ready to change the world, and we need that.

—Interview, *Vanity Fair*, December 27, 2007

❦

I am desperate for change—now, not in 8 years or 12 years, but right now. We don't have time to wait. We need big change—not just the shifting of power among insiders. We need to change the game, because the game is broken. When I think about the country I want to give my children, it's not the world we have now. All I have to do is look into the faces of my children, and I realize how much work we need to do.

—Campaign speech, Londonderry, New Hampshire,
October 20, 2007

❦

I am proud of my country, without a doubt. I'm a girl who grew up in a working-class neighborhood in Chicago. . . let me tell you, of course I'm proud. Nowhere but in America could my story be possible.

—*The View*, June 18, 2008

Barack is going to make mistakes. But, see, the beauty of Barack making mistakes is that he's not going to be so stubborn that he can't admit that he's making mistakes and he can't look at another way of approaching things.

—Interview, *Larry King Live*, February 11, 2008

∾

So tonight, in honor of my father's memory and my daughters' future—out of gratitude to those whose triumphs we mark this week, and those whose everyday sacrifices have brought us to this moment—let us devote ourselves to finishing their work; let us work together to fulfill their hopes; and let us stand together to elect Barack Obama president of the United States of America.

—Democratic National Convention, Denver, Colorado, August 25, 2008

∾

[D]uring the first campaign, one of my jobs as my husband's spouse was to travel around the country and really listen to women. We held small discussion groups, [and] there were voices that were new to me: the voices of military spouses, many of them women, and veterans. . . . I was overwhelmed by their challenges, and the notion that we as a country don't even know that these women exist, because we live in a country where one percent of the population protects the rights and freedoms of the other 99 percent of us. I thought that if I had the opportunity to serve as First Lady, I was going to use this platform to be their voice.

—Interview, *Glamour*, May 2015

See, that's why he's running—to end the war in Iraq responsibly, to build an economy that lifts every family, to make sure health care is available for every American, and to make sure every child in this nation has a world-class education all the way from preschool to college. That's what Barack Obama will do as president of the United States of America.

—Democratic National Convention, Denver, Colorado, August 25, 2008

∽

[Hillary] has been phenomenal. From the minute after this was done, she has always been just cordial and open. I've called her. I've talked to her. She's given me advice about the kids. We've talked at length about this kind of stuff, how you feel, how you react. She has been amazing. She is a real pro and a woman with character.

—Interview, *Larry King Live*, October 8, 2008

FIRST LADY

What I owe the American people is to let them see who I am so there are no surprises. I don't want to be anyone but Michelle Obama. And I want people to know what they're getting.

—Interview with Oprah Winfrey, *O Magazine*, April 2009

❧

I spent the first few months in the White House mainly worrying about my daughters, making sure they were off to a good start at school and making new friends before I launched into any more ambitious work.

—Interview, *Good Housekeeping*, January 2019

❧

When they set off for their first day at their new school, I will never forget that winter morning as I watched our girls, just 7 and 10 years old, pile into those black SUVs with all those big men with guns. And I saw their little faces pressed up against the window, and the only thing I could think was, what have we done?

—Democratic National Convention, Philadelphia, July 25, 2016

Watching my mother transition into this house, knowing where she comes from—an even poorer than working-class upbringing—to seeing her standing on the Truman Balcony and representing this country as the First Grandmother, I mean, those moments are just as surreal as watching the girls go through it.

—Interview, *People*, December 19, 2016

❧

When I traveled internationally, grandma was there. When I wasn't home at the end of the day, grandma was there. When the kids were still little and they needed to have someone be with them in school. I mean, you think about my girls were being driven around in a motorcade of three cars with at least four grown adults with guns in each of those cars. And I just thought that that's an unnatural way for a little second grader to go to school. Well, mom would ride in the car with her to make it feel like a regular carpool.

—Interview with Gayle King, *CBS This Morning*,
November 14, 2018

❧

I specifically did not read other first ladies' books because I didn't want to be influenced by how they defined the role. I knew that I would have to define this role very uniquely and specifically to me and who I was. So, I came in thinking about who I wanted to be in this position and who I needed to be for my girls.

—United State of Women Summit, Washington, D.C.,
June 14, 2016

We learned in our household that there was nothing you couldn't talk about and that you found humor in even some of the toughest times. I want to bring that spirit of warmth, openness, and stability to my task.

—Interview, *Vogue*, March 2009

❧

I think people respond differently when there's a little humor, and people feel like you're opening—you're making yourself vulnerable. Then you seem less like the First Lady and more like a neighbor, a friend.

—American University conference at the National Archives, Washington, D.C., September 16, 2016

❧

I want people to know me, know Michelle, Michelle Robinson Obama, not the First Lady. In every interaction I have had with anybody who's had some connection with me, I have tried to be authentically myself. And in order to do that, I learned that I have to do things that I authentically care about. Because if I fundamentally, deep down have a belief in the cause . . . then I'm going to be excited about it. That excitement is going to be conveyed to the people that I'm trying to reach.

—United State of Women Summit, Washington, D.C., June 14, 2016

So if there's one message I want to send to parents today, it's this: We have a voice. We have a voice. And when we come together and use that voice, we can change the way companies do business. We can change the way Congress makes laws. We can transform our schools and our neighborhoods and our cities. And today, I want to urge everyone to keep using that voice, keep standing up and demanding something better for our kids.

—"Let's Move!" anniversary event, Alpharetta, Georgia, February 9, 2011

And I've watched so many kids come through those gates and really be in that space—picking tomatoes with me in the garden, getting to sit in and have tastings at the state dinner, being invited to watch *Hamilton*. . . . [J]ust watching their eyes just experiencing things that really only the privileged get to experience, but having it be kids and people who would never believe they would set foot in that house.

—United State of Women Summit, Washington, D.C., June 14, 2016

And when I come across many little black girls who come up to me over the course of this 7½ years with tears in their eyes, and they say: "Thank you for being a role model for me. I don't see educated black women on TV, and the fact that you're First Lady validates who I am. . . ."

—Interview, *Variety*, August 23, 2016

And today, as First Lady, whenever the term "authentic" is used to describe me, I take it as a tremendous compliment, because I know that I am following in the footsteps of great women like Maya Angelou. But really, I am just a beginner—I am baby-authentic.

—**Maya Angelou's memorial service, Winston-Salem,
North Carolina, June 7, 2014**

❧

I am moved by this community—moved deeply. Because when we talk about pride of country, when we talk about citizenship, when we talk about all the things we want—we want a strong defense, we want to beat back terrorism—all of this is resting on the shoulders of this one community. As I said, 1 percent of the country who is stepping up to serve to protect the freedoms of us all. And we can't just talk strong defense if we're not taking care of these men and women—not just during their service, but after.

—**Addressing men and women serving in the military,
American University conference at the National
Archives, Washington, D.C., September 16, 2016**

❧

This is a unique spotlight, and my goal has been to make sure I don't waste it. That's really been the thing. I mean, every day I wake up, it's like, good lord, please make sure that I'm being relevant, that I'm having impact, that I'm making the difference, particularly in the lives of young people.

—**South by Southwest Music Festival,
Austin, Texas, March 16, 2016**

[W]hat I realized over the years is that home is where we are. You know? And the White House happened to be our home for eight years. But we took all that love and energy, and we just moved it to another house. It's still there. And . . . that's the part of life that's important.

—*Interview with Gayle King*, CBS This Morning, *November 14, 2018*

I don't have the stressful job. He does. You know, I have the privilege of working on the issues that I choose and the issues that I feel most passionate about. It's been a privilege.

—Interview, NPR, April 17, 2012

∾

And that's really why Jill Biden and I started Joining Forces—because we are proud of all of you. I can't say it enough. Working with our military community has been the biggest honor of my life. This is a proud moment for me. We wanted to rally all of Americans to serve you as well as you serve this country every single day. And I am thrilled by everything that we've achieved together over the past five years to ensure that you and your families have the jobs you deserve, the benefits you've earned, and the honor and support of our nation, that you know that we love you.

—At the commissioning of the USS *Illinois*, Groton, Connecticut, October 29, 2016

∾

But Jill is much more than a partner. She is one of my dearest friends. And, as Jill said, we're family. This is my girl right here. We have laughed together. We have been silly together. We have cried a lot. We've been there for each other as much as we can throughout this amazing journey. And Jill is not just brilliant, but she is kind. She is very funny. And she is one of the strongest people I know. I love and admire her with all my heart.

—At the Joining Forces Capstone Reception with Dr. Jill Biden, November 14, 2016

Being your First Lady has been the greatest honor of my life, and I hope I've made you proud.

—**Final remarks as First Lady, School Counselor of the Year Ceremony, Washington, D.C., January 6, 2017**

❧

And when I leave here, there will be another platform. I don't know what that will feel like, but I will still have that same sense of obligation and responsibility that my parents taught me growing up—that to whom much is given, much is expected.

—**South by Southwest Music Festival, Austin, Texas, March 16, 2016**

POLITICS

Politics was never ever anything I would have chosen for myself. . . . It was very difficult being married to a man that felt like politics was his destiny.

—Interview, NPR, November 9, 2018

Every time Barack came to me with the idea of running for an office, I was just like, "Please don't do this. Pick another career. You're gifted. Y'all went to college. You got a law degree. Can't you do anything else besides this?" There's so many ways to save the world. But every time I had to think to myself, that approach is selfish. Because I knew I was married to someone who was gifted and someone who could contribute.

—Interview with Gayle King, *CBS This Morning*,
November 14, 2018

The country has the responsibility—the right and the responsibility to critique their president. That's part of the job. So you know, you take in what you need to and you keep the stuff that doesn't apply out and you keep working every day.

—Interview with Barbara Walters, ABC News,
November 26, 2010

I love that for Barack, there is no such thing as "us" and "them"—
he doesn't care whether you're a Democrat, a Republican, or none
of the above . . . he knows that we all love our country . . . and he's
always ready to listen to good ideas . . . he's always looking for the
very best in everyone he meets.

—**Democratic National Convention, Charlotte,
North Carolina, September 4, 2012**

❧

[I]f I had to pick the man I'd want to be in politics, the kind of
person that we seek out in this country, somebody who's honest
and sincere, and smart as a whip, he would be the person that I
would pick and that's always been why I followed him into these
escapades. . . because I would feel guilty to think that because of
me that somebody like him didn't do what this country needed.
And I still feel that way. And I'll feel that way until the job is
done. But that's up to the American people.

—**Interview with Barbara Walters, ABC News,
November 26, 2010**

❧

I want someone with the proven strength to persevere, someone who
knows this job and takes it seriously, someone who understands that
the issues a president faces are not black and white and cannot be
boiled down to 140 characters.

—**Democratic National Convention,
Philadelphia, July 25, 2016**

We want a president who values and honors women, who teaches our daughters and sons that women are full and equal human beings worthy of love and respect.

—Campaign speech, Winston-Salem, North Carolina,
October 27, 2016

❧

[F]or so long, America has been a model for countries across the globe, pushing them to educate their girls, insisting that they give more rights to their women. But if we have a president who routinely degrades women, who brags about sexually assaulting women, then how can we maintain our moral authority in the world? How can we continue to be a beacon of freedom and justice and human dignity?

—Campaign speech, Manchester, New Hampshire,
October 13, 2016

❧

People who are truly strong lift others up. People who are truly powerful bring others together. And that is what we need in our next president. We need someone who is a uniting force in this country. We need someone who will heal the wounds that divide us, someone who truly cares about us and our children, someone with strength and compassion to lead this country forward.

—Campaign speech, Manchester, New Hampshire,
October 13, 2016

If people are wondering, yes, Hillary Clinton is my friend. . . . She has been a friend to me and Barack and Malia and Sasha. And Bill and Chelsea have been embracing and supportive from the very day my husband took the oath of office.

—Campaign speech, Winston-Salem, North Carolina,
October 27, 2016

❦

Because here's the truth: Either Hillary Clinton or her opponent will be elected president this year. And if you vote for someone other than Hillary, or if you don't vote at all, then you are helping to elect her opponent. So I want you all to think about that for a minute. Think about how you'll feel waking up on November the 9th if that happens.

—Campaign speech, Phoenix, Arizona,
October 20, 2016

❦

I went to bed. I don't like to watch the political discourse; I never have. I barely did with him. Once you do what you can do, then you rest easy. It was in the hands of the American people. Anything that I felt about the election I said and I stand by. This is our democracy, and this is how it works. We are ready to work with the next administration and make sure they are as successful as they can be. Because that's what's best for this country.

—Discussing the November 2016 election night, interview,
People, December 9, 2016

I am sick of all the chaos and the nastiness of our politics. It's exhausting and, frankly, it's depressing. I understand wanting to shut it all out.

—*Campaign speech, Las Vegas,*
September 24, 2018

Politics

I have never had the passion for politics. I just happen to be married to somebody who has the passion for politics, and he drug me kicking and screaming into this arena. Just because I gave a good speech and I'm smart and intelligent doesn't mean that I should be the next president. That's not how we should pick the president. That's been our problem. We're very shortsighted about how we think about selecting the commander-in-chief.

—39th Annual Simmons Leadership Conference, Boston, April 5, 2018

For me, deciding to run for office would be like deciding to live on the moon. Politics is just not the place for me. I'm not cut out to make a life there. It's too chaotic, too messy, and the tribalism and nastiness aren't something I want to experience day-to-day. I'm someone who prefers order and calm, and politics doesn't offer that.

—Interview, *Ebony*, December 2018

For the eight years Barack was president, it was like having the "good parent" at home. The responsible parent, the one who told you to eat your carrots and go to bed on time. And now we have the other parent. We thought it'd feel fun, maybe it feels fun for now because we can eat candy all day and stay up late, and not follow the rules.

—39th Annual Simmons Leadership Conference, Boston, April 5, 2018

No one knows what it's like to be commander-in-chief. They don't know the hardship, the dangers, the information he gets. Everyone thinks they know, but they don't. So, when people tell lies about the commander-in-chief, I know they don't understand what they're doing. When other people repeat it, they don't understand, either. What I wanted to explain is that when you do this, you escalate the risks. You put the person who's in charge of the welfare of this country and his family at risk. We have to stop it.

—Interview, *New York Times*, November 20, 2018

∿

Now, I hope there are some people in the audience who want to be president of the United States, because we need you. We need you out there. We need good, smart, decent people with strong values and strong morals who want to go into politics. So I would encourage all of you to consider a life in public service. Even if you want to make money, find a way to help somebody. Find a way to turn your blessings into something powerful that affects the lives of others. Because that's how we keep this country strong.

—South by Southwest Music Festival,
Austin, Texas, March 16, 2016

You have to be analytical, you have to be smarter than your advisers in order to do that. So, those are the women that we need to seek out. Not just the women who have passion, and move us, and make us feel good. That's what we look for. You know, this notion that we want our president to make us feel a certain way is important, yes—but it is more important that they understand the issues not just in this country, but around the world.

—39th Annual Simmons Leadership Conference,
Boston, April 5, 2018

FAMILY

My mother's love has always been a sustaining force for our family, and one of my greatest joys is seeing her integrity, her compassion and her intelligence reflected in my own daughters.

—Democratic National Convention, Denver, Colorado,
August 25, 2008

❧

My mom is an incredibly intelligent and insightful person about life in general. From the time we could talk, she talked to us endlessly about any- and everything with a level of openness and fearlessness that made us believe that we were bright enough to engage with an adult, that we were worthy enough to ask questions and to get really serious answers—and she did it with a level of humor.

—Interview, *Essence*, May 2009

❧

My dad was our rock. Although he was diagnosed with multiple sclerosis in his early 30s, he was our provider, our champion, our hero. As he got sicker, it got harder for him to walk, it took him longer to get dressed in the morning. But if he was in pain, he never let on. He never stopped smiling and laughing. . . . He and my mom poured everything they had into me and Craig. It was the greatest gift a child can receive: never doubting for a single minute that you're loved, and cherished, and have a place in this world. And thanks to their faith and hard work, we both were able to go on to college.

—Democratic National Convention, Denver, Colorado,
August 25, 2008

Family

Here is the thing that I will tell men out there, for a girl to have strong men in her life, like I had, a father who loved me, a brother who adored me and cared for me, [it] made me stronger. I want to make sure that men understand the importance of male role models in the life of a strong girl and my brother has been my hero from day one.

—Interview with Robin Roberts, ABC News, Chicago, November 13, 2018

⮑

In those days, fast food was a special treat. My brother and I got pizza a few times a year—as a reward for good grades when report cards came out. No one in my family believed in eating out, especially not my grandmother. I will never forget the time when my brother and I begged her to get us takeout burgers and fries for lunch. We were shocked when she finally agreed. And as we sat excitedly waiting for our burgers to arrive, and I swear this is true, my grandmother brought out a can of peas. And, much to our horror, she promptly served us two scoops each. My grandma failed to grasp one of the key benefits of takeout for kids, and that was no vegetables! Fast food or not, my grandma believed in feeding her family a balanced meal at every meal.

—"Let's Move!" anniversary event, Alpharetta, Georgia, February 9, 2011

My grandmother lived around the corner, my grandfather lived two blocks away, they each lived with aunts and uncles. My paternal grandparents lived maybe ten blocks away. It was rare to see a family where one person was trying to cook, clean, watch the kids, do it all. You always had a community.

—Interview with Oprah Winfrey, *O Magazine*, April 2009

∾

I had a very stable, conventional upbringing, and that felt very safe to me. And then I married a man who came from a very different kind of upbringing. He didn't grow up with a father; his mother traveled the world. So we both came to this marriage with very different notions about what children need, and what does a couple need to be happy. So I had to give up some of my notions, and so did he.

—Interview, *Vanity Fair*, December 27, 2007

∾

We were so young, so in love, and so in debt.

—Democratic National Convention, Charlotte, North Carolina, September 4, 2012

Family

[T]he Barack Obama I know today is the same man I fell in love with 19 years ago. He's the same man who drove me and our new baby daughter home from the hospital 10 years ago this summer, inching along at a snail's pace, peering anxiously at us in the rearview mirror, feeling the whole weight of her future in his hands, determined to give her everything he'd struggled so hard for himself, determined to give her what he never had: the affirming embrace of a father's love.

—Democratic National Convention, Denver, Colorado,
August 25, 2008

✑

I love our daughters more than anything in the world, more than life itself. And while that may not be the first thing that some folks want to hear from an Ivy League–educated lawyer, it is truly who I am. So for me, being Mom-in-Chief is, and always will be, job number one.

—Commencement address, Tuskegee University, Alabama,
May 9, 2015

✑

I come here as a mom whose girls are the heart of my heart and the center of my world—they're the first thing I think about when I wake up in the morning, and the last thing I think about when I go to bed at night.

—Democratic National Convention, Denver, Colorado,
August 25, 2008

My father, Fraser Robinson, taught me to work hard, laugh often, and keep my word. Every day, I see @barackobama instilling those same values in our girls. #HappyFathersDay to dads everywhere who shape who we are—and who will always live on in our hearts.

—@MichelleObama, Instagram, June 17, 2018

❧

We have a wonderful marriage. But it takes work.

—Interview with Gayle King, *CBS This Morning*, November 14, 2018

❧

For a period in my life, I thought the help I needed had to come from Barack. It wasn't that he didn't care, but he wasn't there. So I enlisted moms and babysitters and got help with the housecleaning, and I built that community myself.

—Interview, *Vanity Fair*, December 27, 2007

❧

So when people ask me whether being in the White House has changed my husband, I can honestly say that when it comes to his character, and his convictions, and his heart, Barack Obama is still the same man I fell in love with all those years ago.

—Democratic National Convention, Charlotte, North Carolina, September 4, 2012

Well, because people are invested in us as a perfect couple, I thought it was important to make sure that couples know that marriage is hard. Let me start by saying this. I love my husband, and we have a great marriage. But great marriages require work. And great marriages have rough spots.

—*Interview,* All Things Considered, *NPR,* *November 12, 2018*

She's an active presence in their lives, as well as mine, and is instilling in them the same values that she taught me and my brother: things like compassion, and integrity, and confidence, and perseverance—all of that wrapped up in an unconditional love that only a grandmother can give.

—On her mother Marian Robinson, TED Talk, Elizabeth G. Anderson School, London, April 2, 2009

❧

I say this to my kids now, this is one of the greatest lessons that my mother taught me, is that children—you aren't raisin' babies. They're only gonna be cute and little for a little while. But then they grow up and they have to be adults in the world. And everything we do as a parent with our children, we're preparing them for adulthood.

—Interview, "Becoming Michelle: A First Lady's Journey with Robin Roberts," November 11, 2018

❧

I try to have no absolute nos. I love French fries, I like a good burger, and I like pie. And that's okay. I would be depressed if I felt I could never eat the things that I love. I also don't want my girls to be obsessed about food. We don't have a "no junk food" rule—I just want them to think about their choices. When my older daughter asks, "Can I have pie?" I'll say, "Did you have it yesterday? Well, what do you think?" And she'll come to the conclusion that, you know, you're right, I shouldn't eat pie every night.

—Interview, *Prevention*, September 2009

And I am very proud of those two and how they've managed this situation and how they have continued to be themselves, regular little girls just trying to figure it out. And as all mothers do, you breathe that sigh of relief that you didn't mess up your kids. And every day I cross my fingers and hope that I'm doing right by them, and I'm providing them with a good foundation so that they can be great people.

—United State of Women Summit, Washington, D.C.,
June 14, 2016

We are finding each other again. We have dinners alone and chunks of time where it's just us—what we were when we started this thing: no kids, no publicity, no nothing. Just us and our dreams.

—Interview, *People*, November 14, 2018

Thank you @barackobama for 26+ years of love, trust, and respect—for being a man who always lifts up and honors me and our wonderful girls. Each day I'm with you, I'm reminded of what a treasure you truly are to us all.

@MichelleObama, Twitter, October 3, 2018

HAPPINESS AND SUCCESS

Our life before moving to Washington was filled with simple joys . . .
Saturdays at soccer games, Sundays at grandma's house . . . and a
date night for Barack and me was either dinner or a movie, because
as an exhausted mom, I couldn't stay awake for both.

—Democratic National Convention, Charlotte,
North Carolina, September 4, 2012

❧

You know, happiness for me really is when my kids are good and
when my family is whole. . . . My happiness is measured against
theirs—when they're in a good place, I feel really good.

—Interview, *Prevention*, September 2009

❧

After I had Malia, I began to prioritize exercise because I realized
that my happiness is tied to how I feel about myself. I want my
girls to see a mother who takes care of herself, even if that means I
have to get up at 4:30 so I can do a workout.

—Interview with Oprah Winfrey, *O Magazine*, April 2009

❧

Exercise is really important to me—it's therapeutic. So if I'm ever
feeling tense or stressed or like I'm about to have a meltdown, I'll
put on my iPod and head to the gym or out on a bike ride along
Lake Michigan with the girls.

—Interview, *Marie Claire*, October 22, 2008

One of the things I realized is that if you do not take control over your time and your life, other people will gobble it up. If you don't prioritize yourself, you constantly start falling lower and lower on your list, your kids fall lower and lower on your list.

—United State of Women Summit, Washington, D.C.,
June 14, 2016

❧

So I have freed myself to put me on the priority list and say, yes, I can make choices that make me happy, and it will ripple and benefit my kids, my husband, and my physical health. That's hard for women to own; we're not taught to do that.

—Interview, *Prevention*, November 2009

❧

First and foremost, I wear what I love. That's what women have to focus on: what makes them happy and what makes them feel comfortable and beautiful. If I can have any impact, I want women to feel good about themselves and have fun with fashion.

—Interview, *Vogue*, March 2009

❧

De-stressing now, it's like spending time with good friends to good music and laughter. Laughter is a huge de-stressor.

—Howard University, Washington, D.C.,
September 1, 2016

And that's what it means to be your true self. It means looking inside yourself and being honest about what you truly enjoy doing. Because graduates, I can promise you that you will never be happy plodding through someone else's idea of success. Success is only meaningful—and enjoyable—if it feels like your own.

—Commencement address, Oregon State University, Corvallis, Oregon, June 17, 2012

❧

Your success will be determined by your own fortitude, your own confidence, your own individual hard work. That is true. That is the reality of the world that we live in. You now have control over your own destiny. And it won't be easy—that's for sure. But you have everything you need. Everything you need to succeed, you already have, right here.

—TED Talk, Elizabeth G. Anderson School, London, April 2, 2009

❧

Success isn't about how your life looks to others, it's about how it feels to you. We realized that being successful isn't about being impressive, it's about being inspired. And that's what it means to be true to yourself.

—Commencement address, Oregon State University, Corvallis, Oregon, June 17, 2012

Anyone who has achieved anything in life knows that challenges and failures are necessary components of success. They know that when things get hard, that's not always a sign that you're doing something wrong, it's often a sign that you're doing something right. Because those hard times are what shape you into the person you're meant to be.

—BET's "Black Girls Rock!" event, Newark, New Jersey,
March 28, 2015

∾

One thing I want you all to remember is that failure is an important part of success. Nobody up here went a straight line to success. There are bumps and slip-ups and embarrassments that you think you will never overcome. Everyone has had it, from the president on up or down, whichever way you look at it.

—Howard University, Washington, D.C.,
September 1, 2016

RACE AND RACISM

As a child, my first doll was Malibu Barbie. That was the standard for perfection. That was what the world told me to aspire to. But then I discovered Maya Angelou, and her words lifted me right out of my own little head.

—Maya Angelou's memorial service, Winston-Salem,
North Carolina, June 7, 2014

❧

[W]e could probably go into any room of black women, or people of color, or people who grew up in poor communities, or rural communities, and you'd ask them, "Has anybody ever told you you couldn't?" And everyone would raise their hand.

—Interview with Gayle King, *CBS This Morning*,
November 14, 2018

❧

What I learned is that I have to be in control of my image, my voice. I have to be thoughtful. And also, because I'm a black woman, I am toned. There's a different judgment about my facial expressions. If I'm too vigorous in my reply, people will think I'm being uppity. You're judged in your community because you're not black enough. And then you get out in the world, and you're too black. . . . So that period in my life told me I have to define me on my own terms before others define me, you know?

—Interview, *All Things Considered*, NPR,
November 12, 2018

My experiences at Princeton have made me far more aware of my "Blackness" than ever before. I have found that at Princeton no matter how liberal and open-minded some of my White professors and classmates try to be toward me, I sometimes feel like a visitor on campus; as if I really don't belong.

—from Michelle Robinson's senior thesis, "Princeton-Educated Blacks and the Black Community," 1985

❧

The shards that cut me the deepest were the ones that intended to cut. . . . Knowing that after eight years of working really hard for this country, there are still people who won't see me for what I am because of my skin color.

—30th Anniversary of the Women's Foundation of Colorado, Denver, July 25, 2017

❧

[M]y heart goes out to the parents, because we all as parents understand the tragedy of that kind of loss. . . . I think we all need, as a country, to continue to talk about these issues, to understand our communities and the challenges that we face, which are different and unique depending upon where you live. . . . It is complicated. It takes time. It takes openness. It takes compassion. It takes patience. And it takes a lot of work. So we should all be ready to roll up our sleeves and keep doing that work.

—On the death of Trayvon Martin, interview, NPR, April 17, 2012

But no matter what you do, the point is to never be afraid to talk about these issues, particularly the issue of race. Because even today, we still struggle to do that. Because this issue is so sensitive, is so complicated, so bound up with a painful history. And we need your generation to help us break through. We need all of you to ask the hard questions and have the honest conversations, because that is the only way we will heal the wounds of the past and move forward to a better future.

—*Topeka School District Senior Recognition Day.*
Topeka, Kansas, May 17, 2014

We know that today in America, too many folks are still stopped on the street because of the color of their skin—or they're made to feel unwelcome because of where they come from, or they're bullied because of who they love.

—Topeka School District Senior Recognition Day,
Topeka, Kansas, May 17, 2014

❧

[W]e can't control other people's expectations. Some folks are going to see a Black boy with a hoodie and think he's a thug. Some folks are going to see a Black girl speaking up in class and think she's too loud or too bossy. . . . The good news is that none of this is insurmountable. We've got to help our kids believe in their own stories—every part of those stories, the ups and the downs. We've got to show them that their strength is found in what's so often perceived by society as a weakness.

—Interview, *Ebony*, December 2018

❧

So like many of you, I believe that education is the single most important civil rights issue that we face today. Because in the end, if we really want to solve issues like mass incarceration, poverty, racial profiling, voting rights, and the kinds of challenges that shocked so many of us over the past year, then we simply cannot afford to lose out on the potential of even one young person. We cannot allow even one more young person to fall through the cracks.

—Black History Month "Celebrating Women of the Civil Rights Movement" panel, Washington, D.C., February 20, 2015

I love you all. I believe in you all. And I am confident that you all
will shine brightly, lighting the way for generations of girls to come.

—BET's "Black Girls Rock!" event, Newark, New Jersey,
March 28, 2015

❧

[I]n the end, we know our history, and we know that there will
always be challenges and obstacles, but we also know that what
we're dealing with today is nothing—nothing—compared to the
violence, discrimination, and hatred that folks faced decades ago.

—Commencement address, Jackson State University,
Jackson, Mississippi, April 23, 2016

HARDSHIP, HOPE,
VALUES, AND VIRTUE

I want you to understand that every scar that you have is a reminder not just that you got hurt, but that you survived. And as painful as they are, those holes we all have in our hearts are what truly connect us to each other. They are the spaces we can make for other people's sorrow and pain, as well as their joy and their love so that eventually, instead of feeling empty, our hearts feel even bigger and fuller. So it's okay to feel the sadness and the grief that comes with those losses. But instead of letting those feelings defeat you, let them motivate you. Let them serve as fuel for your journey.

—Commencement address, Martin Luther King Jr. Preparatory High School, Chicago, June 9, 2015

∽

And, graduates, more than anything else, that will be the true measure of your success—not how well you do when you're healthy and happy and everything is going according to plan, but what you do when life knocks you to the ground and all your plans go right out the window. In those darkest moments, you will have a choice: Do you dwell on everything you've lost? Or do you focus on what you still have, and find a way to move forward with passion, with determination, and with joy?

—Commencement address, Oregon State University, Corvallis, Oregon, June 17, 2012

Now, my Dad didn't live to see me in the White House. He passed away from complications from his illness when I was in my twenties. And, graduates, let me tell you, he is the hole in my heart. His loss is my scar. But let me tell you something, his memory drives me forward every single day of my life. Every day, I work to make him proud. Every day, I stay hungry, not just for myself, but for him and for my mom and for all the kids I grew up with who never had the opportunities that my family provided for me.

—Commencement address, Martin Luther King Jr.
Preparatory High School, Chicago, June 9, 2015

❧

You should never view your challenges as a disadvantage. Instead, it's important for you to understand that your experience facing and overcoming adversity is actually one of your biggest advantages.

—Commencement address, City College of New York,
June 3, 2016

❧

It is our fundamental belief in the power of hope that has allowed us to rise above the voices of doubt and division, of anger and fear that we have faced in our own lives and in the life of this country. Our hope that if we work hard enough and believe in ourselves, then we can be whatever we dream, regardless of the limitations that others may place on us. The hope that when people see us for who we truly are, maybe, just maybe, they, too, will be inspired to rise to their best possible selves.

—Final remarks as First Lady, School Counselor of the Year Ceremony,
Washington, D.C., January 6, 2017

[Y]ou may not always have a comfortable life. And you will not always be able to solve all of the world's problems at once. But don't ever underestimate the importance you can have because history has shown us that courage can be contagious, and hope can take on a life of its own.

—Keynote address, Young African Women Leaders Forum, Soweto, South Africa, June 22, 2011

Hope is what keeps our better angels alive. It's been the driving force behind everything we've achieved these last eight years, and it's been at the heart of my life and my husband's life since the day we were born.

—Campaign speech, Phoenix, Arizona, October 20, 2016

So that's my final message to young people as First Lady. It is simple. I want our young people to know that they matter, that they belong. So don't be afraid—you hear me, young people? Don't be afraid. Be focused. Be determined. Be hopeful. Be empowered. Empower yourselves with a good education, then get out there and use that education to build a country worthy of your boundless promise. Lead by example with hope, never fear. And know that I will be with you, rooting for you and working to support you for the rest of my life.

—Final remarks as First Lady, School Counselor of the Year Ceremony, Washington, D.C., January 6, 2017

That's the choice Barack and I have made. That's what has kept us sane over the years. We simply do not allow space in our hearts, minds, or souls for darkness. Instead, we choose faith—faith in ourselves, in the power of hard work. Faith in our God, whose overwhelming love sustains us every single day. That's what we choose.

—Commencement address, Jackson State University, Jackson, Mississippi, April 23, 2016

❧

We learned about dignity and decency—that how hard you work matters more than how much you make . . . that helping others means more than just getting ahead yourself. We learned about honesty and integrity—that the truth matters . . . that you don't take shortcuts or play by your own set of rules . . . and success doesn't count unless you earn it fair and square. We learned about gratitude and humility—that so many people had a hand in our success, from the teachers who inspired us to the janitors who kept our school clean . . . and we were taught to value everyone's contribution and treat everyone with respect.

—Democratic National Convention, Charlotte, North Carolina, September 4, 2012

❧

I have learned that as long as I hold fast to my beliefs and values— and follow my own moral compass—then the only expectations I need to live up to are my own.

—Commencement address, Tuskegee University, Tuskegee, Alabama, May 9, 2015

But when you come from a family like mine, that's what you do. You make the most of what you've got. You use all that good common sense and you don't make excuses. You work hard, and you always finish what you start. And no matter what, you give everybody a fair shake, and when somebody needs a hand, you offer yours.

—*Commencement address, Eastern Kentucky University, Richmond, Kentucky, May 11, 2013*

It's the belief, as my husband often says, that if any child goes hungry, that matters to me, even if she's not my child. If any family is devastated by disease, then I cannot be content with my own good health. If anyone is persecuted because of how they look, or what they believe, then that diminishes my freedom and threatens my rights as well. And in the end, that sense of interconnectedness, that depth of compassion, that determination to act in the face of impossible odds, those are the qualities of mind and heart that I hope will define your generation. I hope that all of you will reject the false comfort that others' suffering is not your concern, or if you can't solve all the world's problems, then you shouldn't even try.

—Keynote address, Young African Women Leaders Forum,
Soweto, South Africa, June 22, 2011

Dignity had always gotten us through. It was a choice, and not always an easy one, but the people I respected most in life made it again and again, every single day: There was a motto Barack and I tried to live by, and I offered it that night from the stage: *When they go low, we go high.*

—*Becoming*

SPEAKING TO
YOUNG PEOPLE

There is no boy at this age that is cute enough or interesting enough to stop you from getting your education. If I had worried about who liked me and who thought I was cute when I was your age, I wouldn't be married to the President of the United States.

— "Let Girls Learn" event, New York City,
September 29, 2015

❧

I always tell young girls, surround yourself with goodness. I learned early on how to get the haters out of my life. You've got to just sort of surround yourself with people who uplift you, who hold you up.

—United State of Women Summit, Washington, D.C.,
June 14, 2016

❧

What matters is that you believe in your own potential, and that's for sure. You have to believe in you first. Because people will try to tear you down, I guarantee you that. There will never be a point at which people will 100 percent be cheering you on. So when you hit those barriers in life, all you have is your belief in yourself. That's all you have to fall back on. What also matters is how hard you're willing to work. Because none of this is easy—and it's not supposed to be. Because then everybody could do it, right?

—*Hidden Figures* film screening, Washington, D.C., December 15, 2016

And to all our students going to college, I wish you all the very, very best of luck. You got a President and a First Lady who are behind you all every step of the way. Just remember, when you hit a barrier, that's when you grow. So don't let that shut you down— because we've all had our trials and tribulations. We've all failed big in some way, shape or form. The question isn't whether you fail, it's how you get up and move on.

—Jazz Festival Workshop, Washington, D.C.,
April 29, 2016

∽

But if you don't have that parent—that mother, that father—then you've got to find it. You've got to find those people. Because they're out there. I tell my mentees . . . there is somebody out there who loves you and who is waiting to love you, and you just have to find them. And that means you have to make room for them. And if you're surrounded by a bunch of low-life folks who aren't supporting you, then there is no room for the people who do love you.

—United State of Women Summit, Washington, D.C.,
June 14, 2016

∽

I want you to ask those basic questions: Who do you want to be? What inspires you? How do you want to give back? And then I want you to take a deep breath and trust yourselves to chart your own course and make your mark on the world.

—Commencement address, Tuskegee University,
Tuskegee, Alabama, May 9, 2015

So for all of you sitting here with those doubts in your head—because those whispers of doubt, they stay with you for a very long time— ignore them. Brush them off. And just do the work. Do the work. And it's the doing of the work that gets you through. It's not what other people think of you. And I still carry that with me today as First Lady of the United States, because there are people who don't think I should be doing that, either. And it's been about eight years now.

—Howard University, Washington, D.C., September 1, 2016

❧

[W]e're a country that believes in our young people—all of them. We believe that every single child has boundless promise, no matter who they are, where they come from, or how much money their parents have. We've got to remember that. We believe that each of these young people is a vital part of the great American story. I can't say that enough.

—National Arts and Humanities Youth Program Awards, Washington, D.C., November 15, 2016

❧

So I tried to be a serious student and not procrastinate, but I was still somebody that would be described as somebody who liked to have fun, too. . . . And that's why I think it's important [to] hold on to your authentic self, even in this experience, as you grow and achieve. It's like, remember who you always were, where you came from, who your parents were, how they raised you. Because that authentic self is going to follow you all through life, so make sure that it's solid so it's something that you can hold on and be proud of for the rest of your life.

—Howard University, Washington, D.C., September 1, 2016

Do not ever let anyone make you feel like you don't matter, or like you don't have a place in our American story—because you do. And you have a right to be exactly who you are. But I also want to be very clear: This right isn't just handed to you. No, this right has to be earned every single day.

—Final remarks as First Lady, School Counselor of the Year Ceremony, Washington, D.C., January 6, 2017

When you leave here, who are you going to share this knowledge with? A younger cousin, a sister or brother, a neighbor? All of us are mentors. You're mentors right here and now. And one of the things I've always done throughout my life, I have always found that person, that group of people that I was going to reach my hand out and help bring them along with me. . . . So think about how you're going to take this experience and carry it into your communities, into your families.

—Love and Happiness Concert: Student Workshop,
Washington, D.C., October 21, 2016

∾

These are not issues that go away in a presidential term. They don't go away in a lifetime. And why I work so much with young people is that you all are going to be the ones who take on these issues. You're going to be the one that carries these things over the finish line—whether it's climate change, or global education, or health and fitness, you all are the ones who are going to have to do that work. And I want you all to feel good about yourselves, and be empowered, and feel prepared to take on the leadership roles that we're going to need to have you—we're going to hand this stuff over to you, and we're going to have your backs while you're doing it.

—South by Southwest Music Festival,
Austin, Texas, March 16, 2016

Right now, you need to be preparing yourself to add your voice to our national conversation. You need to prepare yourself to be informed and engaged as a citizen, to serve and to lead, to stand up for our proud American values and to honor them in your daily lives. And that means getting the best education possible so you can think critically, so you can express yourself clearly, so you can get a good job and support yourself and your family, so you can be a positive force in your communities.

—Final remarks as First Lady, School Counselor of the Year Ceremony, Washington, D.C., January 6, 2017

So, graduates, while I think it's fair to say that our Founding Fathers never could have imagined this day, all of you are very much the fruits of their vision. Their legacy is very much your legacy and your inheritance. And don't let anybody tell you differently. You are the living, breathing proof that the American Dream endures in our time. It's you. So I want you all to go out there. Be great. Build great lives for yourselves. Enjoy the liberties that you have in this great country. Pursue your own version of happiness. And please, please, always, always do your part to help others do the same.

—Commencement address, City College of New York, June 3, 2016

THE WIT AND WISDOM OF
MICHELLE OBAMA

He's always asking: "Is that new? I haven't seen that before." It's like, Why don't you mind your own business? Solve world hunger. Get out of my closet.

—Interview, *New York Times*, March 20, 2009

❧

That's the thing about being the First Lady: You try to catch your friends up on what's happening in your life, and they're like, We know—we read it in the paper.

—Interview with Oprah Winfrey, *O Magazine*, April 2009

❧

I remember one parent-teacher conference at the lower school, and Barack went, and there were SWAT guys on top of the roof of the school. And Malia was like, "Dad, really? Really? Do they really have to be up there?" And it's like, yeah, honey, they do. Let's just keep walking. Just keep going.

—American University conference at the National Archives, Washington, D.C., September 16, 2016

❧

I am the First Lady but my mother is like, "When is Craig coming?" I'm like, "I live in the White House. What more do I have to do?"

—On her brother Craig Robinson, interview with Robin Roberts, ABC News, Chicago, November 13, 2018

I want to walk down a street. I want to sit in a yard that is not a national park. I do want to drop into Target. . . . I've heard so many things have changed in Target! I tell my friends they're going to have to give me a re-entry training for like, okay, what do you do at CVS now? How do you check out? It's like I've been living in a cave.

—On returning to civilian life after the White House,
United State of Women Summit,
Washington, D.C., June 14, 2016

❧

What I have never been afraid of is to be a little silly, and you can engage people that way. My view is, first you get them to laugh, then you get them to listen. So I'm always game for a good joke, and I'm not so formal in this role.

—Interview, *Variety*, August 23, 2016

❧

One of the lessons that I grew up with was to always stay true to yourself and never let what somebody else says distract you from your goals. And so when I hear about negative and false attacks, I really don't invest any energy in them, because I know who I am.

— Interview, *Marie Claire*, October 22, 2008

Every day, you have the power to choose our better history—by opening your hearts and minds, by speaking up for what you know is right.

—Topeka School District Senior Recognition Day,
Topeka, Kansas, May 17, 2014

❧

[W]hen it comes to social media—there are just times I turn off the world, you know. There are just some times you have to give yourself space to be quiet, which means you've got to set those phones down. You can't be reading all that stuff. . . . that's like letting somebody just walk up and slap you, you know? You would never do that. You would never just sit there and go, slap me in the face and I'm good with it. No. So why would you open yourself up to that?

—United State of Women Summit, Washington, D.C.,
June 14, 2016

❧

[A]s we move forward in life and we get access to these seats of power, these tables of power, I want you to look around and make sure there's diversity at the table. Because you don't come up with the right answer if everyone at the table looks the same and thinks the same and has the same experience—you never come up with the best answer.

—*Hidden Figures* film screening, Washington, D.C.,
December 15, 2016

I think in my 40s, I started feeling very comfortable in my own skin. Motherhood helps, marriage helps—those learning curves that force you to be better. And my hope is that my 50s will hone that. I never consider myself a finished project.

—Interview with Oprah Winfrey, *O Magazine*, April 2009

❧

[I]t takes taking the time to know who you are to be able to deal with the onslaught of negative messages that you're bound to get. So for me, I came into this with a pretty clear sense of myself. And some of that comes with age. Some of that comes with experience. Some of that comes from being fortunate enough to have been raised by a loving mother, strong, focused, and a father who loved me dearly. So I fortunately came into this situation with a really clear sense of who I was. So when you hear the smack-talking from outside the world, it's easy to sort of brush that off. Because I know who I am.

—United State of Women Summit, Washington, D.C.,
June 14, 2016

❧

Part of why I knew my book had to be done, and done well, is because it's a rare moment in history that a black woman gets to tell her own story. Success stories look a certain way: they're male; they're white; they're wealthy. That's what power looks like because we've been taught that. And we question stories that are different from the ones we're used to. How many stories do you know where millions of people are hearing about strong women, told by a woman, and hearing her pain?

—Interview, *New York Times*, November 20, 2018

The question that I hate most that we ask of young people is, "What are you going to be when you grow up?" And the truth is, I still don't know, and I'm 45 years old. All I know is that it's important for you to be true to yourselves, not to worry too much about what other people are going to think or make of your choices, because everyone will question what you do and tell you you should've done it the other way.

—*Howard University, Washington, D.C.,*
February 11, 2009

Just try new things. Don't be afraid. Step out of your comfort zones and soar, all right?

—Howard University, Washington, D.C.,
September 1, 2016

❧

If you're a Democrat, spend some time talking to a Republican. And if you're a Republican, have a chat with a Democrat. Maybe you'll find some common ground, maybe you won't. But if you honestly engage with an open mind and an open heart, I guarantee you'll learn something. And goodness knows we need more of that, because we know what happens when we only talk to people who think like we do—we just get more stuck in our ways, more divided, and it gets harder to come together for a common purpose.

—Commencement address, Eastern Kentucky University,
Richmond, Kentucky, May 11, 2013

❧

So one message that I want to leave you with tonight is this: The secret to everything in life—every aspiration, every opportunity—is education. It's education. There is nothing more important than being serious about your education.

—BET's "Black Girls Rock!" event, Newark, New Jersey,
March 28, 2015

[W]hat I've learned is that I'm best at doing things that have a deep meaning for me. How I decide what to advocate is personal. And I tell young girls to start with their own passions. There isn't just one way. Politics is a way. It's never been anything I wanted to do. But I am an advocate.

—Interview, *New York Times*, November 20, 2018

∽

And remember that in difficult times, we don't give up. We don't discard our highest ideals. No, we rise up to meet them. We rise up to perfect our union. We rise up to defend our blessings of liberty. We rise up to embody the unwavering hope that keeps us going—day after day, generation after generation. That is the power of hope.

—Campaign speech, Phoenix, Arizona, October 20, 2016

QUOTES ABOUT
MICHELLE OBAMA

I have always looked up to Michelle because she has been able to do things that I couldn't do emotionally, psychologically or physically. I think she is amazing.

—Marian Robinson, interview, *Essence*, May 2009

༄

Most people who meet my wife quickly conclude that she is remarkable. They are right about this—she is smart, funny, and thoroughly charming. She is also very beautiful. . . . Often, after hearing her speak at some function or working with her on a project, people will approach me and say something to the effect of, "You know I think the world of you, Barack, but your wife . . . wow!" I nod, knowing that if I ever had to run against her for public office, she would beat me without much difficulty.

—Barack Obama, *The Audacity of Hope*

༄

Of all the things that I'm most proud of, and my sister has done a whole lot of things, a lot of initiatives, but one of the biggest things that was apparent to our family was how she made family imperative within our own sort of family. Even though she was busy doing all these wonderful things, we had Thanksgiving at the White House, we had Fourth of July at the White House and our entire family felt a part of being in such a historical environment.

—Craig Robinson, interview with Robin Roberts, ABC News, Chicago, November 13, 2018

To have risen to the heights that she has risen to before she even became First Lady—from being a lawyer to her public service dedication in Chicago—are things you just don't shake off. All of those are character-building experiences. You can tell when you speak with her that she grew up in a space where family, community, and making a difference were everything. And she carried all of those experiences right into the East Wing. Everyone who met her knew that they were dealing with someone very, very real.

—Isha Sesay, interview, CNN, January 19, 2017

She is the smartest, toughest, funniest, best friend that I could ever hope for, and she's always had my back.

—Barack Obama, *Washington Post*, December 11, 2006

Michelle always arrived at her own opinion. It wasn't the women's position; it wasn't the black position. Michelle would take all the information and process it through her experience, her beliefs, her value system, and she would arrive at the Michelle Robinson position or opinion.

—Beverly Thomison-Sadia, Princeton classmate, in "Michelle in High Cotton," by Benilde Little in *The Meaning of Michelle: 16 Writers on the Iconic First Lady and How Her Journey Inspires Our Own*

She has a comforting spirit about her, and she makes you feel included, listened to, and important. That's part of her strength and her legacy: As smart and inspirational as she is, she is also completely relatable. And she's not afraid of fashion. . . . Not since Jackie Kennedy have we seen a first lady use her wardrobe to quietly express what she stands for.

—*Jason Wu in* Courage Is Contagious:
And Other Reasons to Be Grateful
for Michelle Obama

She just knew the private practice of law was not sufficiently satisfying, and she was willing to walk away from a huge salary potential and all the trappings of power that go along with it

—Valerie Jarrett, *Vanity Fair,* December 27, 2007

She's something of a force of nature—one of the rare few who are truly present with whomever she's talking to. Whether it's a veteran, a child, a working mother, or movie star, she treats everyone the same, with respect and full attention.

—J. J. Abrams

Michelle showed how to shape the role to her own interests and needs, combining a meaningful policy agenda and political role with her determination to keep her family whole and sane.

—Peter Slevin, *Michelle Obama: A Life*

She's letting women know that the word *appropriate* has changed. She isn't afraid to make a mistake, and to be stylish you have to be willing to make a mistake.

—Michael Kors in *Everyday Icon: Michelle Obama and the Power of Style* by Kate Betts

The irony is that Michelle Obama makes it look easy precisely because she is complicated. Simultaneously flawless and imperfect, she brilliantly navigates opposing forces. And in the tension we can all see ourselves.

—Tiffany Dufu, "On Being Flawlessly Imperfect," in
*The Meaning of Michelle: 16 Writers on the Iconic
First Lady and How Her Journey Inspires Our Own*

❧

There are no rules for her. She's done everything in her own way. She's just a straight shooter. Every time she speaks it always seems from the heart, it seems genuine. That's hard to do.

—Jenna Lyons in *Everyday Icon: Michelle Obama
and the Power of Style* by Kate Betts

❧

Eight years of watching Michelle Obama as a *person*, not just relegated to doing "woman things," provided an antidote to all the false representations of black women that have inundated us for centuries—images that don't represent the reality, or the humanity, of who we are as black people. Of who we are as people. And then to have her name prefaced by two things that are rarely associated with black women—"first" and "lady"— well, it shattered everything.

—Tracee Ellis Ross in *Courage Is Contagious: And Other Reasons
to Be Grateful for Michelle Obama*

Obviously I couldn't have done anything that I've done without Michelle. You were asking earlier what keeps me sane, what keeps me balanced, what allows me to deal with the pressure. It is this young lady right here . . . Not only has she been a great First Lady, she is just my rock. I count on her in so many ways every single day.

—Barack Obama, interview with Oprah Winfrey, May 2, 2011

Michelle LaVaughn Robinson, girl of the South Side—for the past 25 years, you have not only been my wife and mother of my children, you have been my best friend. You took on a role you didn't ask for and you made it your own, with grace and with grit and with style and good humor. You made the White House a place that belongs to everybody. And the new generation sets its sights higher because it has you as a role model. So you have made me proud. And you have made the country proud.

—President Barack Obama, Farewell Address,
Chicago, January 10, 2017

CHRONOLOGY

January 17, 1964 — Michelle LaVaughn Robinson is born to Fraser C. Robinson III and Marian (Shields) Robinson in Chicago, Illinois. She joins brother Craig Robinson, who was born in April 1962.

1981 — Graduates from Whitney M. Young Magnet High School in Chicago. She was a member of the National Honor Society and served as student council treasurer.

1985 — Graduates from Princeton University with a bachelor's degree in Sociology and a minor in African-American studies.

1988 — Graduates from Harvard University with a Juris Doctor degree.

1988 — Accepts position as associate attorney at Sidley & Austin, a Chicago law firm.

June 1989 — Meets Barack Obama, who is working as a summer associate at Sidley & Austin. The two begin dating later in the summer.

March 6, 1991 — Fraser Robinson dies at the age of 55 from complications from multiple sclerosis.

July 1991 — Leaves law firm and begins working for Chicago Mayor Richard Daley.

July 31, 1991 — Becomes engaged to Barack Obama.

October 3, 1992 — Marries Barack Obama at Trinity United Church of Christ in Chicago.

1992–1993 — Works as Assistant Commissioner of Planning and Development in Chicago's City Hall.

1993 — Becomes founding Executive Director of Public Allies Chicago, an AmeriCorps national service program.

1996–2002 — Serves as Associate Dean of Student Services for the University of Chicago and Director of the University Community Service Center.

July 4, 1998 — Gives birth to Malia Ann Obama.

June 10, 2001 — Gives birth to Natasha (Sasha) Obama.

2002–2005 — Serves as Executive Director for Community Affairs at University of Chicago Hospitals.

November 2, 2004 — Barack Obama is elected U.S. senator for Illinois.

2005–January 2009 — Serves as Vice President for Community and External Affairs at the University of Chicago Medical Center.

August 25, 2008 — Addresses Democratic National Convention in Denver, Colorado.

November 4, 2008 — Barack Obama is elected the 44th president of the United States and the first African-American president.

January 20, 2009 — Becomes the First Lady of the United States and the first African-American First Lady.

February 2010 — Launches "Let's Move," a national campaign aimed at addressing childhood obesity.

April 2011 — Launches "Joining Forces," a national veterans' campaign, with Dr. Jill Biden.

June 2011 — Travels to Africa for a week. Speaks on issues including health, education, and youth leadership. Visits Nelson Mandela at his home.

May 2012 — Publishes her first book, *American Grown: The Story of the White House Kitchen Garden and Gardens Across America*.

September 4, 2012 — Addresses Democratic National Convention in Charlotte, North Carolina.

May 2014 — Launches "Reach Higher," a national initiative aimed at encouraging young people across America to continue their education past high school.

March 2015 — Launches "Let Girls Learn," a global girls' education initiative to help girls go to school and stay in school across the globe.

July 26, 2016 — Addresses Democratic National Convention in Philadelphia, famously declaring " . . . our motto is, when they go low, we go high."

October 13, 2016 — Delivers a speech at a campaign event for Hillary Clinton in Manchester, New Hampshire, wherein she issues a powerful rebuke to Donald Trump in response to his vulgar comments about women from a taped interview with Billy Bush of *Access Hollywood* in 2005.

January 6, 2017 — Gives final address as First Lady and remarks, "Being your First Lady has been the greatest honor of my life, and I hope I've made you proud."

July 2018 — Launches "When We All Vote," a voting initiative aimed at ensuring that every American exercises his or her right to vote.

October 2018 — Launches the Global Girls Alliance, an organization that will support approximately 1,500 girls-education groups around the world.

November 13, 2018 — Publishes her memoir *Becoming*, which becomes the best-selling hardcover book of 2018.

December 2018 — Michelle Obama is voted the most admired woman of 2018, according to a December 2018 Gallup poll.